AF080637

An Ode For You

A collection of heartfelt dedicated short poems

Solasta Noori

Ukiyoto Publishing

All global publishing rights are held by

Ukiyoto Publishing

Published in 2023

Content Copyright © Eunice Jessica C. Arellano

ISBN 9789358467192

All rights reserved.

No part of this publication may be reproduced, transmitted, or stored in a retrieval system, in any form by any means, electronic, mechanical, photocopying, recording or otherwise, without the prior permission of the publisher.

The moral rights of the author have been asserted.

This book is sold subject to the condition that it shall not by way of trade or otherwise, be lent, resold, hired out or otherwise circulated, without the publisher's prior consent, in any form of binding or cover other than that in which it is published.

www.ukiyoto.com

Acknowledgement

First, I would like to thank Ukiyoto Publishing for publishing this book. I would always be thankful for giving me an opportunity to be one of your authors. Next, Miss Janette A. Roble, my class adviser, thank you so much for being our adviser. Miss, you taught us more about what the lessons in classrooms would be taught. You taught us values that we need in our lives as we continue our journey ahead. I look up to how strong you are Miss and I'm beyond grateful for your trust to me too Miss Janz. All I can say to everything is thank you so much Miss, *thank you*.

Third, my family who always supports me in every way they can. Lastly, I would like to mention some of the people behind this poem that I wrote, they have been part of my highschool journey and some have been with me since we were kids. Isabelle Allende once said, "Write what should not be forgotten." So, I wrote my gratitude to you this way, thank you for being part of my journey...

Cris Mae Salibongcogon, Ferah Mae Apas, Cielo Cagulang, Darren Joyce Pepito, Kaye Ivan Aguipo, Kysha Elle Faith Apas, Tricia Mae Maceda, Genevie Cabatingan, Karren Montegrande, Reya Baloro, Mary Lyn Alapre, Jazmine Jade Achumbre, Alexa Bacalla, Miel Thea Batayola, Noryl Arranchado, Lea Bianca Anoos, Aimee Rose Yano, Geisha Recamara, Genebabe Balansag, Maria Jane Nicole Bate, Marque Ann Angtud, Sophia Roque, Deserie Seldora, Jennifer Burlaos, Althea Cogo, Kherbie John Aguipo, Cassidy Paradiang, Khricia Kris Abiso, Jeansly Barral and to all my friends.

All the best to all of us on our next journey. Good luck!

Contents

If life was a movie	1
Its been a while	2
Dearest	3
Sunshine	4
Youth	5
To the girl who loves purple	6
Mi Esperanza	7
Walk of life	8
Queen	9
My magic and sunshine	10
Brave soul	11
Avid fan	12
Muse	13
Solace	14
With you	15
Karen	16
Tease	17
Surprising	18
Brave	19
What meets the eye	20
Aphrodite	21
Oh, youth	22
Pave the way	23
Ever so confident	24
Twenty Fifteen	25
Art	26
Mother	27
Eonnie	28

Dear, Dreamer	29
Enamored	30
Sophia	31
Achiever	32
Chase	33
Damsel	34
Charm	35
Talent	36
Your day	37
After goodbye	38
About the Author	*39*

If life was a movie

If life was a movie, it would be nice to pause and stay at the best moments.

If life was a movie, it would be nice to pause and take a break from all the torments.

If life was a movie, it would be nice to rewind the happiest moments all over again.

If life was a movie, it would be nice to rewind and undo your mistakes.
.

If life was a movie, it would be nice to know the ending.

If only life was a movie, it would be nice to move forward so that you could only go to the best part.

But life was no movie.

You can't pause, rewind nor forward anything.

But if life was a movie you're the best part.

Trust me, you are the very best part of everything.

The plot twist that I never saw coming.

It's been a while

It's been a while when I realize, we're closer than anyone else.

It's been a while when I realize, you're too near yet too far.

It's been a while when I realize, my heart's torn apart in seeing you from afar.

It's been a while when I realize, you're giving me a farewell feels.

It's been quite a while that I realize, we're like asymptomatic lines.

The ones who get closer and closer…but can never be together.

'Cause the more we get closer to our dreams, the farther we get to each other.

Dearest

Among all the shades in my eyes you are the brightest.
Keep your vibrance.
I'll be here always happy, of your existence.
If you feel down, don't let it make you frown.
Don't overanalyze.
Just let the situation realize.

Sunshine

The brightest sunshine in your eyes glows ever so bright.

Holding a light that could illuminate the darkest night.

Smiles that were ever so vibrant, swept hearts and became an immortalized art.

Youth

It is to be back on the time when we are young.
Those carefree hearts, and lasting laughs.
Those fluttery feeling, that seems beyond lasting.
It was our season of blossoms.
Hearts and the worlds collide, and the fate is not ours to decide.
The season where everything seems fine.
Oh, how nice it would be back in time when we were young.

To the girl who loves purple

When she was a child.

She enjoyed the soft breeze and the green leaves.

The scent of the warm summer, and the tasty peanut butters.

The three o'clock sun, the bubbles that seem to run, the blue skies and pies.

She looked at them today once again, and dreamt the same dream again.

The coffee that brightens her day.

The warm smile that used to greet her every day.

The undeniable pressure and that common things that reassure.

How far did those simple pleasures go?

It's so far for her to hold onto.

How much did she run chasing the sun?

It seemed too near yet too far for her to have.

When did that warm summer breeze turn into a scorching heat?

When did that tasty peanut butters become bitter appetizers?

What happened to the three o'clock sun that seemed to glow for no one?

Why do it seem that the bubbles pop, like the seething kettle in the countertop?

How does the blue sky turn into a gray sky?

Where's the pie that can put her into a smile?

Mi Esperanza

You're the most favorite poem, I'll always read.
You are like the language, that I want to keep learning.
Every words was dedicated to you.
You're unaware of it, I know.
You've destroyed all my walls.
And all I did was to keep you know about it all.

Walk of life

Missing your presence, I always admire your kind heart and pure soul.
We've been through the phases of life.
Childhood to adolescence to adult life.
Whatever you do, I'll be rooting for you.
Silently yet loudly.
Don't think you're ever behind in the walk of life.
We're walking on our own timeline.
And you're never late.
You are walking your own great fate.

Queen

A heartfelt gratitude for you.

We've been part of each other's up's and down's.

We've been each other's clowns, when one of us are feeling down.

As brave like some knight, don't ever let anyone dim your light.

Or if someone does?

They should hide with all their might.

I got you, like you did to me too.

One must treat you like a Queen.

As they should be!

You're my hope and lifeline, got each other's back every time.

Let's go to our dreams and succeed!

As what we have vowed to each other to achieve.

My magic and sunshine

Like magic you came suddenly…almost blindingly.
We are polar opposites.
You're the sun shining.
I'm just the moon illuminating.
You're funny, while I take jokes too seriously.
I'm an introvert and you're an extrovert.
Funny, how we click somehow.
It was me, finding our opposite personality to click maybe.
And it's true!
Because of you I saw youth.
The world you made me see, was as vibrant as who you are.
You're my season of magic.
The magic and sunshine.
And you made me helplessly fall in love
with life again.
I can't thank you enough.

Brave soul

Your name sounds as sweet as you are.
A good friend, worthy of love.
You will always have my thanks.
Keep doing you're best!
You're sweet and brave than you think.
Let me tell you this.
You're braver than you thought you are.
You've conquered the obstacles in your way.
You're worth praising.

Avid fan

You're the artist I look up to.
I am in awe in how talented you are.
You can breathe life in your art.
The photos of your characters seem to be real.
I'm rooting for you like an avid fan.
Since day one.

Muse

You were once the muse; it was not on the news.

You were once his important dear.

But memories seem too far yet too near.

So, never forget, that someone won't never ever forget.

You were a dear, proven by the words written

Solace

Never feel lonely, you are one of a kind of lovely.

You'll start a new journey.

Never feel lonely of the solitude of the first morning.

You'll never start alone, you'll start again, but this time you'll start from experience.

And attract the positive friends… yet again.

So, smile, the solitude would not last a day.

With you

You're quite the strong one,
Never like anyone.
Quite unique…but not eccentric.
Face things head on, so focus on,
You'll see at the end of the tunnel.
The hope…it's been waiting for you.
The whole time.
We're with you.

Karen

K- Kind, that's you.

A - Adorable, whether in appearance or your attitude.

R- Resilient, still strong despite the situation.

E- Energetic, still have the energy to keep fighting.

N- you Never give up at everything.

You keep on every day. You're brave!

Keep fighting you'll see how your fighting spirit leads you.

Tease

One, here's someone.
Two, but not for you.
Three, you're lucky and also unlucky.
Four, what's fate for?
Five, does the feelings still thrive?
One, two, three…fate is a tease thee.

Surprising

You amaze me sometimes, in more ways than one.
You manage to awe me with your brilliance.
Keep it up, you're quite silent.
But surprisingly resilient.

Brave

Your name was a symbolic flower and one of the favorite Disney character.

You are vibrant and charming.

And brave…to some extent.

Hoping for you keep your vibrance from fading.

What meets the eye

You're a kind soul, you're uniquely beautiful.
Never feel ashamed of physical beauty.
You're more than what meets the eye.
With a heart worth appreciating.

Aphrodite

You're indeed a gift, the world has her spotlight on you.
You held your head high keep that.
So, whenever life through you on the rough path.
You can hold unto that.
It will lead you to the end of the stage.
And awe the audience gazes, with your resilience.

Oh, youth

Being young is lovely cherish it, make memories.
Always keep the vibe happy.
One day you'll make everyone proud.
Claim it, you're getting there.
The moment has been waiting for you.

Pave the way

First, congrats to you, you've surpassed the journey.
We've yet to face the new a challenge…big changes.
But never feel wary.
You've come a long way.
You're going to pave the way.

Ever so confident

Never fading confidence ever since we were kids.
You've come a long way.
Your confidence is amusing.
It really awes me how easy for you amaze people.
Trust me, it takes you far.
Keep being confident.
My more than a decade friend.

Twenty Fifteen

Surprising how long we've known each other… since 2015.
The kid who was once us, looking at us now, is surely proud.
We're almost there, you've come a long way.
The world is smiling for your journey in succeeding.

Art

Your name means art, indeed your grace was art.

Soft spoken, heart of gold, your shy nature is one that makes you beautiful.

You have a gentle soul, the world's going to appreciate it if you let them see.

Mother

Vibrant in nature

Resilient pillar

Protective.

A mother your kids are thankful for.

Eonnie

How many episodes left there?
How many seasons you're watching?
How many *oppa's* have you chosen?
Really seriously, thanks to your hobby.
You've become diversely linguistic.
You're a good friend
an obedient member…sometimes you
forget our paper.
But still, continue to be charming.

Dear, Dreamer

You're a dreamer, a creative soul, a doting friend.
You're dreamer side had me realize…how the world needs dreamers.
Keep dreaming dear dreamer.
And the world will dream with you.

Enamored

You're heart is strong, you're a nice person.
Trust me, people see how nice you are.
Keep your heart strong.
People are enamored by your nice nature.

Sophia

As soft as your name, your beauty has amazed a lot of hearts.

Your grace may have awed some poets, to write a romance of the century.

You're one of a kind of beauty, not only physically.

Your heart has mirrored this beauty.

Achiever

You work hard like nobody else, making you achieve far.
You didn't give up!
And you did achieve the greatest heights…of your dreams.
You're getting there.
Keep going.
Let's all be a success to the dreams we've promised.

Chase

You have a big heart full of kind love, and wisdom.

Rest your anxious heart.

The right one will never run.

When time is right it will eventually come.

Run for your dreams!

Chase your goals.

Make your love ones proud.

Damsel

A woman like you deserves more than the world.
The people around appreciate your existence.
They might be shy to say it, but you know it.
A dreamer by heart,
An introvert who loves art.
Just like what they said.
Smile always.
You're a brave soul, who conquered those silent battles.
This time, I'm rooting in your every win.
Looking up to how brave you are.

Charm

You're charmingly cute and friendly.
Never be anxious of the challenge.
You're vibrant personality will change your destiny.
You'll attract the right persons in your life.
You're braver than you thought you would be..

Talent

You're talented and gifted.
You're talent has amaze people.
Including me for example.
Keep it up!
You'll see how amaze the people are.
Believe on your own charm.

Your day

Energetic and vibrant, you're simply attracting.
You've got confidence that amaze the masses.
Never let anyone ruin your day.
Enjoy it!
It's all yours anyway.

After goodbye

We are in the same book, on the same chapter but
I cannot say the same about the ending.
It's been a while was it not?
Everything goes back to square one.
All had continued their lives the way it was before,
The same way that we do.
But moments came back on the silence of this midnight.
Old conversation in my head resumes,
Where only fluttering feeling my heart consume,
On this same hour where the trust bloomed.
"After the goodbye, time seemed to fly."
How do we go back to the way exactly before when we have seen
The brightest colors and hues?

About the Author

Eunice Jessica Arellano

Solasta Noori also known as *Eunice Jessica Arellano* in real life is an eighteen-year-old National Book Development Board registered writer who resides in Cebu, Philippines. She writes romance stories and short poetries, some of her works can be found on Wattpad and Tappy. She's also one of the contributors of Ukiyoto Publishing anthology project Magkasintahan 2.0. Her work can be found in the volume III of the anthology.

www.ingramcontent.com/pod-product-compliance
Lightning Source LLC
LaVergne TN
LVHW041558070526
838199LV00046B/2033